Dangerously Deep

Dangerously Deep

A E S S Y N C E

ISBN: 978-0-578-06690-5

Printed in the United States of America

Published 7, December 2010

Photography: Cornelius James Lewis
Hair: Denika Huggins

LCCN/PCN: 1-259646821

To that special man from my yesterdays,

I'll never forget you.

Happy Birthday!!!

Acknowledgements

I have to devote total praise to my Lord and Savior Jesus Christ for showing me the mercy and many blessings that he allows me to see, and also for those unseen. I know that everything happens for a reason and he has given me strength to carry on and pull through after every storm.

To my Mother for carrying me into this world, and for constantly pushing me and inspiring me to finally PUBLISH!!! I did it! We did it! Together! I love you so much and I pray for you everyday. • To my Grandmother, who from day one supported me and believed in everything I ever did, you are my heart. I wouldn't be half of what I am without you and I believe that. • To Shawon, I can't wait to see you blossom into the beautiful intelligent woman you are destined to become, Love Big Sis ☺ .

I know that I have been blessed to have a select few of trusted friends who I consider to be extended family and you all know who you are. My Cassandra, you are the rock solid in my life. You are everything I think a woman should be and I am thankful to have you in my corner and I trust you completely, I love you. • To my Connie Con and Kayla Kay, you are my inspiration that faith in God, love, and happily ever after's do come true ☺ • Tiffany, if the world were filled with more people who were understanding, loving, and compassionate like you it would be such a better place. You were there to hold my hand from day one when putting up with me wasn't so easy, and I thank you for listening to me drag on and on about what's his name every night LOL! I love you. • Denika, the woman who keeps my hair flowing and glowing, nobody knows my kitchen like you, LOL. I'd be lost without you ☺ • Constantine, you were there during some of the lowest times to help me let my hair down and drown my sorrows. You've been an awesome friend to me all these years. • To Anna, Brinda, and Marilyn, I can't forget you. Every late night lecture, tough love lashing, and testimonials of your own battles in love and life, I heard you and I appreciate it. • All of you women have endured and have truly inspired me to fight and pull through myself. I know that no journey is ever traveled alone and without you helping me and guiding me throughout this trip I would've never made it as smoothly. You guys keep me believing in me and I love y'all women! ☺

To the fans who've been supportive of me and rooting for me, I thank you all from the bottom of my heart for making my dreams what they are today. I love each and every one of you. You are my confidence to do and share everything that I am no matter the distance.

Lastly, I have to recognize my 9th grade avid teacher at Cedar Grove High School, Ms. Melvina Jordan. I remember it like it was yesterday, reading to you my words and you finding yourself within my teenage love affair. You are my biggest fan, and I love you endlessly! • Also thanks to Morgan Hudson-Davis and the entire family for the constant push and motivation. Especially Mama Hudson-Davis ☺ .

And to all of the girls who've been at this point, just know this isn't the end... Never give up!

Contents

INTRODUCTION

DEAR LOVE

Upon seeing him, my eyes froze and my breath shortened. Instantly my soul was set on fire to a degree that was new to me and dangerous. In such a short time, I fell in love with him. An emotion I had never experienced before, yet came to me as second nature- *I fell in love with him*. No feeling meant more than that and my duty was to respect it.

Admittedly, I was in love with everything about him before I even got a chance to know him. But I was exploring him and it was a journey that fulfilled me to the highest rank. Each new challenge I encountered along my joyride to being his only queen, seemed to only strengthen me to stay and love him that much harder and more deeply than the day before. His presence overpowered me and I was captured by his eyes and the essence of his being. This was dangerous because I had fallen in love with him more than I ever knew how to be in love with myself. The problem was, with a love this strong, pure and faithful, I couldn't see beyond him. I couldn't see past my love for him. I couldn't see outside of his ideas and suggestions. My staying power fueled by my love of him made me blind and irresponsible. But the one thing that was clear to me all the while, was that it was in fact, love. And I didn't want to escape it.

As I said before, learning more about him only intrigued me to fall more deeply into him. With every day I fell deeper and deeper, it nearly destroyed me to have to leave him behind in the end. Following the verbal, physical, and emotional abuse I suffered, I found my breaking point. What I thought took me so high off the ground ended up only throwing me that much lower beneath it. I was living for this, and I needed it.

Daily I found myself hypothesizing over the many ways he could save me from everything he was doing to me that hurt so bad. I wanted him to catch me crying inside that little corner where no one else could see, and rush over with such swiftness to fix whatever was wrong. To ease the pain, I needed him to take me inside of his arms and tell me, *everything would be okay*. It could all just be so simple. In my mind, if he kept hurting me this bad, eventually he would have to see what he was doing to me and make it feel better. I needed him to take responsibility for the suffering I was enduring and apologize for it. I was confused and thought that this would make him magically become the man that I was struggling to love. Struggling to forgive. And struggling to believe in. I just wanted him to treat me better. Day after day I wanted and I waited, until it finally happened. I grew up.

This is my story.

D E E P :

extending far from downward,

extending well inward from an outer surface,

not superficially within the body,

extending well back from a surface accepted as front,

occurring or located near the outer limits of the playing area,

remote in time or space,

situated well within the boundaries,

being below the level conscious,

in difficulty or distress,

to a great depth,

a vast or immeasurable extent,

Dangerously Deep...Begins

-PART 1-

The Struggle

Real women tell Real stories. Sometimes it gets Real deep. Dangerously, Deep.

DANGEROUSLY DEEP

February 1, 2003

I've tried to fight it, the feeling I feel is deep

But I can never get away from all of the things you do to me

You mean my life, the days beside you couldn't mean to me anymore

And you know what makes it worse every time you walk out that door

You got me... the beat in my heart battling the butterflies

I never wanna know what it's like without you, I never wanna say goodbye

'Cause I can't do it, I'm not gon' do it, I'm just not the woman I wanna be

Without you here, without you next to me... my pain is dangerously

Deep

I've tried to let you go, somehow the sun shines in the way

Standing beside you through the hardest rain seems like the brightest day

You amount the most magnificent days of all my life,

      but days just weren't enough

Because after all these days went by, I've fallen so deep in love

You've got me... the roots of you have grown inside of my heart

The amalgamation inside of me mesmerizes me to see where we are,

      from where we've start

Boy I can't be, 'cause I can't breathe, I'm just not this woman I wanna be

Without you, I'm not gon' do it without you... my pain is dangerously

Deep

I've tried, but you're still in my system, still in my mind

And what I see when I look at you, I'm done with the picking,

      the boy is mine

I cried, but I thanked God for the appearance of you before I died

'Cause what we have, it's not that easy to put together,

      you can't find two you and I's

That's why inside, I'll always feel like I'm your girl, I'm still your woman

And since the last time I saw you it's been something I really wanted

I cannot do it, I will not do it, I'm just not the woman I wanna be

Without you here, without you next to me... my pain is dangerously

Deep

I said my pain is Dangerously... DEEP

              A E S S Y N C E

DEAR GOD

February 1, 2003

Praying, I'll never be the woman who has to leave from by his side
Praying to you, that this is true and nothing we have turns to lies
And I pray, beautiful as we are is what our kids look like, I fantasize
Because I pray that what he does to me will never have to die
Praying, that what we share no other woman can interfere
And I pray, his hands don't let go from touching my hands still right here
Sweet God, what I feel must be what the deepest love is composed
And my sweet God, the love I feel I don't wanna let go

Praying, on hands and knees, I'll never doubt what makes it true
Praying to you, that this must be an angel sent down to me from you
And I pray, I'll always remember the page I said I want my ring to be
Because I pray our love will grow even more than it has for me
Praying, that what we share no other man can tear apart
Because if I couldn't be in love like this the future would break my heart
Sweet God, what I feel must be what the deepest love is composed
And my sweet God, the man I love, I don't wanna let go

Praying, friends and foes so long repugnance so strong for us
Praying to you,
        when everybody trying to tell me that something is wrong with us
And I pray, I need the strength from you, I need all your energy
The day he pops the question I'll wear that white dress down the aisle

and give to him the virginity
I pray, protection for us while forces are disrespecting us
Cover us, put your shield all around us, no fear will come to shelter us
Sweet God, the love I feel is what a pure love must be composed
My sweet, sweet God, the love I treasure most, I don't wanna let go

Praying...
Only you can allow him the understanding to see how much I love him,
and know just how much I want him,
and feel how much I truly care.
I need him.
Don't let him leave away from me.
Please...

A E S S Y N C E

I, LOVE

January 31, 2003

I love... you

In most deepest, implausible ways I never knew

By the most extraordinary, avid ecstasy that a girl had ever been through

I love... you

In the sweetest, unconditional, spectacular way it is

Being the man you are in my life teaching me how to love the way you did

I've fallen, in love... with you

Being a woman before my time

With a passion that still explodes about you running inside my mind

I... love... you...

For the man you are inside exposed, outside and stripped

And I have never in my life felt anything as real, as pure as this

I've fallen, in love... with you

And it's so much, it's so enormous I can't explain

But no matter what they tell me, what I feel for you,

it will always remain the same

'Cause I love... you

And there ain't no man alive who could try to compete

Not for the treasures and the trinkets for the feeling I feel so free

I've fallen, in love... with you

I am in love with your eyes and then your smile

In love with the way you dress, the way you walk,

    I am in love with your style

    I... love... you...

And I won't let no other woman try to come in between

'Cause this is more than I could've fantasized,

    this is more than I could've dreamed

    I ... Love... You...

And when I see you every morning my soul still feels these trembles

It's been so long since we first met but I promise I still remember

    'Cause I... Love... You...

It comes second to no one else, just how much I care for you

I'm always gon' be the one when you turn around being there for you,

    and always helping you

    And I... Love... You

I don't care what mama say, I don't care what my family do

'Cause when I look into your eyes nothing in this world

    could make me as happy as much as you

    'Cause I... Love... You

Go with you everywhere around Atlanta, tell everybody that you got me

That's why I've fallen in love with you and nothing they do can stop me

    I... LOVE... You

                    A E S S Y N C E

BROWN EYES

January 31, 2003

Behold, a little boy with cornrows and his father's brown eyes

I see my whole life far ahead of me standing there at your side

Behold, with all my womanhood and everything in this world I have

I'll keep on loving you with all I got and I won't never look back

So don't let go, it's good for me that you feel deep down inside

When you ride, I'll ride with you and there's nothing we can't survive

I don't see no other man, I don't see no other boy, no other guy

I just see the man I'll never leave always inside your round brown eyes

Behold, a little girl so pretty, her perfectly designed

A little me with a little you and then Beauty became alive

Behold, the softest spot inside a man we see so tough

Boy this is everything and all there is, and don't you try to hold back

      and don't pull the plug

Don't let go,

      my destiny is to love you the best way I know, the best way I can

And when you ride, I'll ride with you, I vow to stand there by my man

And when you touch me and you'll tell me that you love me deep inside

I'll tremble, because everything I am is inside of your round brown eyes

Behold, the passion, the promise, these words are true

I see me in my white wedding dress standing next to you

      in your white tux too, every time that I look at you

Behold, your last name written all over mine, ain't no turning back
You can open your eyes and grab onto the real thing now,

> this is no longer a dream, I'm the actual thing and that's the fact

I won't let go,

> inside that kitchen, I'll cook your steak and your mash potatoes

I'll run your shower,

> I'll rub your shoulders and rub your neck through all these hours

Behold, I am your woman, I feel this love deep down inside
I see the man I'll never leave deep down inside your round brown eyes
Behold...

A E S S Y N C E

10,000 NIGHTS

January 30, 2003

I'll devote 10,000 years, I will cry 10,000 tears
Every little bit would make it worth it just to have you standing here
I will give 10,000 nights, 10,000 days out of my life
If you would hold me in your arms and say everything will be alright
10,000 strands of my undying love I brush into this viscous wind
In hopes it rushes into you and you think everything else makes sense
10,000 lashes of my sight,
  that I see to adore you, that I see to look for you
10,000 times over again
  and I keep coming back to be the woman that took you

I'll devote 10,000 years, I will cry 10,000 tears
Every little bit would make it worth it just to have you standing here
I will give 10,000 nights, 10,000 days out of my life
If you would hold me in your arms and say one day I'll be your wife
For 10,000 anniversaries, 10,000 coats of red rose petals
And I don't know what lies ahead but I'm delighted enough to settle
I would carry your child 10,000 months,
  I would marry you again 10,000 times
'Cause every little bit would make it worth it
  if I held your hand and you held mine

I would write this poem 10,000 times,

I would travel this continent 10,000 times

If I could end up right here with you and be in love with you every time

10,000 strands, 10,000 glands, 10,000 layers from every man

Would never make up the man I see in you

with this ability inside your hands

I'll devote 10,000 years, I will cry 10,000 tears

Every little bit would make it worth it just to have you standing here

I will give 10,000 nights, 10,000 days out of my life

To see you and be here with you, with 10,000 lashes of all my sight

10,010 x 10,010 of all the days of my life...

A E S S Y N C E

UNTIL THEN

I have to be the one when I look inside of your eyes
To hold you and not let go of you and not lose this thing so true inside
I have to be the one when I see myself back in your eyes
To kiss you and tell you how much I missed you
      since we last said our good-byes
I've just gots to be the one when I'm inside your round brown eyes
To feel this way when we stop going around the circle a million times
And I just wanna be the one every time that your eyes are closed
You're dreaming of and you're always thinking of,
      the one that you need most
When you go home to Illinois, just tell me that you'll come back again
Until then, I'll be the girl saving up all my love till the end, until then...

When I close my eyes I'll see you, open my eyes and I'll see you
I don't care what nobody else do, I believe in me and I believe in you
When we both get to the end I'll say I did it to be with you
When we get to the end, I'll say I went through it all to breathe with you
'Cause what you make me feel is true and you keep doing it so good too
So I'll keep doing what I do too and keep on staying in love with you
When you go home to Illinois, just tell me that you'll be back again
Until then, I'll be the girl saving up all my love till the end, until then...

I'll sit here in amazement,

everything I prayed about in a man I see in you

And this is more than amazement,

sucking up all of your presence, you wonderful dream come true

I'll be there for you, I'll care for you,

we got this whole wide world I'll share with you

And I've already picked out these heels that when you come back,

I'm gonna walk in and I'll wear for you...

I have to be the only one you can trust, standing right there at your side

The only rose growing from underneath the concrete after everything died

When you go home to Illinois, just tell me that you'll come back again

Until then, I'll be the girl saving up all my love till the end, until then...

A E S S Y N C E

Now Playing:

Destiny's Child
> STAY

DEEPEST FEAR

January 28, 2003

We look good together, I don't ask myself how, I don't know why
I just know no matter the uncertainty, at the grand finale is you and I
I don't ask when, but please be back, it's so many hours around this clock
Boy it's been hard and it's been long for this I've constantly fought
Because of your presence, I am the woman I never knew I could be
And every time I thought it was finished,
      it was one more chance that you showed me
But the seconds you leave me wondering, the moments I just have tears
Every minute I don't know what to do, every day that goes by,
      my deepest fear...

All that talking from other girls is crazy but it don't faze me
'Cause if I believed everything I heard by now I know that I would be crazy
All that gossip and all that jealousy, I can't let it get to me, people envy
They always wanted to see you leave me from the very beginning
Come back for me, after all this time I promise I just can't love myself
You think I wanna play these games and I'm so sick of this for myself
These seconds you leave me wondering, these moments I just have tears
Every minute I don't know what to do, every day that goes by,
      my deepest fear...

I'll never see the back of your braided head come back,
      you had enough and you walked away

I wanted to come after you but then I cried

'cause I didn't know what to say

Every time I know you gotta do your own thing and it's far away from me,

I fall down

Every time you just don't miss me back,

and you're okay about doing that

I'm trying to get right there, I'm trying to find my way there,

we should be there

So get me there, boy drive me there, come to my house and pick me up

take me out and go everywhere

Come back for me, don't leave me wondering, baby don't bring me tears

Every day that goes by, don't make true my deepest fears...

AESSYNCE

WOMAN SCORNED

January 27, 2003

Times in my angry place, I turned my back to you, I walked away from you

Miss Independent, I planned a future I tried to walk in way of you

And the way that I use to step, I was looking for brighter days

Didn't give a damn till near too late, now you can't stand to see my face

A woman scorned, things will never be the same I already know

I let you go, said it was time that men should reap what they sow

It was the tears running down my face, it was my love there on the line

It was the addiction I felt inside, the broken heart you let be mine

I just couldn't stand no more, I promise, I couldn't take no more shatter

So many things happened that weren't suppose to,

      love didn't seem to matter

Seemed the more I tried to learn, the more you hated the things I knew

Felt like I'd be so much better off

      if I didn't care about anything just as much as you

A woman scorned, I walked away, I wasn't as crazy the day you met me

Now you can't stand to see my face, after everything you regretted me

It was the tears running down my face, it was my love there on the line

It was the addiction I felt inside, the broken heart you let be mine

I felt inside the woman scorned, my heart said yes, my brain said no

And you deserved it, it's time these boys that don't care about nothing

      have to reap what they sow

It was the tears running down my face, it was my pride there on the line

It was the addiction I felt inside, the broken heart you let be mine

The woman scorned, my eyes say stop, every time my lips say go

And you deserved it, it's time these boys that don't have love for nothing

      and nobody else except themselves have to reap what they sow

So many tears ran down my face, it was my pride there on the line

For the addiction so deep inside, the broken heart you let be mine

The woman scorned...

A E S S Y N C E

HELPLESSLY GAVE

January 26, 2003

Sweet dreams of you, nightmares of me, toss and turn until I scream

And every night I fall asleep pretending that you are here with me

It's no longer a fairytale, no longer a hope, I needed you in my life

I let you in, my guard was down, exposed my vulnerable side

You were my half, my knight in shining armor,

      to the young world I crowned you that

I gave you chances after chances, I always thought you'd come back

When I did things because of you that first I said No… never me

I gave in and I did too, stabbing the key through your tires so helplessly

So damn dumb and so damn desperate, thought too much until I crashed

The infatuation span won't last forever, I just wanted to make it last

I gave my all, I gave my love, I gave my soul, I gave my heart

As I cried busting the tinted windows out from inside of your mother's car

I loved you deep, even through times the worse couldn't get no worse

I needed you to promise from here on out

      you wouldn't try to go back to her

I played the fool, admit I did, I did things that first I said No… never me

I gave in and I did too, crying the wolf over you so desperately

Desires and dreams that made me full, somehow you only ignored

And I just cried digging the keys up and down the side of her left car doors

I pushed myself, I exposed myself, I let you be inside my life

And it was all one big fat lie and now I just can't sleep at night

I cried, spraying the bleach on every side of that closet, I swear I did

I woke up to be with you, you were my every passion to live

I broke the rules to be with you every time I said No, it wouldn't be me

I gave in and I did too, over and over so helplessly

Dear God,

Only you can make me stronger than what I am…

I'm helpless…

A E S S Y N C E

TAKE IT

I'd take it, I forgave it, you said you'd never see her no more

The way you turned this thing around, what happened to once remorse

I'd take it, although I hated it, you could've had at least restraint

How you went out to be with that other girl,

   I wanna forgive you but I just can't

I took it, constantly I tried to overlook it, so hard it was

I was understanding, I was forgiving, I was giving the utmost love

I was true to you despite the fact so many times you spoke these lies

I'd take it and I forgave it, holding in every tear deep down inside

I'd take it, remember you said you wouldn't never yell between these walls

But the way you throw everything around, you have no self control at all

I'd take it, although I hated it, I crossed my legs, I closed my mouth

And when everybody told me that I was crazy I let my love for you be loud

I took it, constantly I tried to overlook it,

   it was much more harder than it seemed

I was the one who stuck it through to be the girl still on your team

I was there for you, I was being right there for you, I didn't go nowhere

I forgave it, everyday I'd take it, hoping inside one day you'd care

Now you can't take it, my shoes like Free's,

   everybody said I should've left a long time ago

When you couldn't take having a woman as real as me,

everybody said I should've left your trifling ass a long time ago
I'd take it, although I hated it,
>I just thought one day things was gon' be better
And that's the reason, and I mean the only reason
>that I still tried to be here and ride to stay together
I took it, I overlooked it,
>I stepped to these females and fought for you
Took it like a heavyweight title,
>out of all these girls and I was the only one who got to you
Now you can't take it, you just can't face me,
>you can't look me in my eye
You can't apologize, you just can't empathize, can't you just sympathize,
>for all the pain I have inside...

I just want you to take it, be man enough to take it, because you gave it...

AESSYNCE

SO UNIQUE

January 25, 2003

What we have no one understands, they just see the bad
They can't see good, they can't even grasp the ties we have
They don't know, they don't realize, they just talk so they can talk
And tell you I'm not good enough,
        they fill your head with all these thoughts
I hope you think, one day I can be more than just anything that they say
And I hope you think, that I'll do my part so you won't have to go away
Because I know what's deep inside, no matter what they can't see
What we have is so distinct, what we have is so unique

What we have, no one else can understand, nothing else can compete
And if you give me the chance to show you they'll be wrong about me
So many times I felt it wouldn't matter, no matter how hard I tried
When they told you that I wasn't good enough,
        despite the tears at night I cried
I hope you know my love for you goes beyond what they can say
And I hope you know I'm willing to do my part to make you say you'll stay
Because I know what's deep inside and I'm trying to make you see
What we have is so distinct, what we have is so unique-
I'm trying to make you see, I'll spend my life to make you see
What we have is something special, what we have is... you and me!

AESSYNCE

NOT INSECURE

I'm not insecure,

    but I know what's true is the truth, I know what's real

I don't have no type of low self-esteem

    but it's the stupid way that you make me feel

You make me feel unpretty, you make me feel like coach,

    you take my opinion of me so low

Make me feel not smart enough, make me feel dumb,

    all the time I feel so slow

You make me feel no man could love me

    and no man could want my body

You make me feel like this is it,

    like I can't never get me nobody

But if I could,

    I know that I would have a better somebody else than you

And if I could,

    I know that I wouldn't never waste my time with you

I'm not like the girls in the magazine, I know what's the truth,

    my world is real

And I don't feel no kind of way bad about myself

    it's just the ugly way that you make me feel

You make me feel confused, now I feel broken,

you make me feel no man could stay the time
You make me feel that on the outside and looking in,
 these boys out here ain't trying to pay me no mind
You make me feel that every man will cheat,
 and every man I love will leave
'Cause it's too many girls around here now
 trying to do this thing they do for free
But if one man didn't,
 I know he'd be a better somebody else than there was you
And if he didn't,
 I wouldn't trip and wanna waste all this time I've spent with you

You make me feel like this is nothing, like no man could want my body
You make me feel like this is it and I won't be able to find me nobody
But if I could, I know that he would be a better man than ever was you
And if I could, I'd know right now
 that I don't have to waste my time with chasing you
I'm not insecure, but I know what's true, for me the world is just so real
I don't have low self-esteem it's just the stupid way you make me feel
I'm not insecure, I don't look like those girls, it's true, the mirror's real
And I don't feel no kind of way bad about myself
 but it's the ugly way that you make me feel
I'm not insecure...

A E S S Y N C E

Now Playing:

Vivian Green
>EMOTIONAL
    ROLLARCOASTER

A MISCONCEPTION

January 24, 2003

I never wanted to believe that you didn't never wanna marry me,

    but another day I love you and you didn't give me the ring

I never wanted to believe you'd take it this far,

    if this didn't never mean anything

I never wanted to believe that this was stupid,

    I was bending it over backwards

I never wanted to think after all this time what I was doing,

    that it didn't even matter

I never wanted to believe you didn't want no kids,

    but that's the biggest part of my dream, I want those branches

I could see a little boy who looks like you

    and I think that he would be handsome

The biggest misconception; if I gave you more time

    we would eventually be happy and then move forward

My misunderstanding;

that I could change your mind from messing around with all those whores

I never could've believed that you were always this way

    before I was even the chick with you

I never could've believed that I couldn't cure you,

    I just thought that if I just tried to I could fix you

I never could've walked away back in the day,

but I had no choice the day you did it

And it hurts because I love you

and there is nothing I do can fix it

I never could've believed you hated love,

but another day I love you with nothing back

And now I realize and see no misconception,

boy you ain't never gonna come back

The biggest misconstruction: me changing you,

somehow I was the only one who ever changed

And the biggest mistake: I stayed with you

I thought would ease all the pain

No misunderstanding: when I read that letter she wrote

I just couldn't believe

The final straw on the camel's back,

the deepest misery I never thought could all be happening to me...

I couldn't believe

A E S S Y N C E

DEEPEST THOUGHTS

Your eyes, just like a photographer,

    through you I see myself

Your lips, just like a painter,

    I've become so different since the time that we have met

I'm hearing something and I think I like it,

    it's so... so... def...

Because your love is the microphone,

    now I can finally hear myself

Your hands just like the lightning,

    you touch me I feel thunders

You captured me and boy I like it,

    finally I discover the every wonder

And when I think about it this same way,

    and this is always being the way it's not

Inside of my fantasy...

    inside of my deepest thoughts...

Your voice, just like the spark,

    your steps huge when coming down

Your name is in my mouth,

    and when I let it out how sweet is the sound

Sweeter than a chocolate Hershey kiss,

    I won't stop from kissing you

And I don't wanna limit myself,

    these past days boy I've been here still missing you

Now I can hear it,

    you taking me inside of the softest, unhurried beat

And the vocals that we create on top

    is sinking down into the very insides of me

I'm playing the radio and I love it,

    thinking of us being the way it's always not

Inside of my fantasy…

    inside of my deepest thoughts…

Thinking about it,

    there was Pinkett and there was Payne, now here are you and me

Baby,

    there are these lyrics flowing through every cord inside of me

I think about it,

    your kiss, your lips, your hands to touch

Thinking about you touching my waist right now

    when I'm wearing my sexy stuff

I finally hear it,

    you and me and the slowest unhurried thuggish beat

I can finally feel it, you're touching me

    like a guy could never feel a girl down to where it's deep

When I think about it so good, think about it so long

    and this is being the way that it's always not

Inside of my fantasy… inside of my deepest thoughts…

    Thinking about it…

A E S S Y N C E

EVEN YOU

January 23, 2003

I love you, I adore you, I've been loyal to only you
Through your flaws and your facades, I was always just too true
I said forever, we stayed together through the times that it hurt me
I might be crazy but I love you and that love never deserted me
Told you I don't care about no other girl, as a man you've made mistakes
And I forgave your love for those and I still wanted your love to stay
Told you I am in love with you, I am here, I'm reading this poem for you
And nobody can ever take this love away from me inside, not even you

Because I love you more than words, now I love you more than paper
That's the reason that I've held on to every moment I savor
That's the reason I see your face and this big smile just takes control
And I think about how much happiness I'd be missing out on,
        if you I just didn't never know
That's why I loved you being wrong, I gotta love you when you're trying
I gotta love you until it's right, no matter if I keep on crying
Because I need you, that's why I'm here, I'm reading this poem for you
And nobody can make this feeling just go away, they can't make it fade
        not even you

Even when you say things that you don't mean,
        even when you do things you shouldn't do
It ain't no male and it no female

who's gonna make me stop loving you
Even when half your braids undone,
        and them classic tennis shoes on your feet
I can't help but wanna run my fingers through your hair,
        and admire the man standing in front of me
Even that grill inside your mouth,
        the way you lick your lips when you talk to me
It feels so sweet to me,
        and I can't help but giggle every time that you smile at me
It's something about you, something special,
        they can say what they want, think what they want
This love is everything to me,
        and they can hate it long as they want

Told you I am in love with you, I am here,
        I'm reading this poem for you
And nobody can ever make this go away, can't make it fade from me,
        not even you...

A E S S Y N C E

GET IT

January 22, 2003

I don't get it, you always knew how bad you really, really had me
I don't see it, that chick I saw you with to be IT just as bad as me
And I don't hear it, why you tell me our thing happening had to stop
What peach you know as sweet as me down to the very last drop
'Cause what you mean, I'm not worth it, I'm not the time that I put in
What are you saying, you never wanted it to go this far, we're too deep in
You had me easily, loved you completely, it was immediately, so deeply
That I don't understand it now when you tell me that you don't need me

I don't get it, you showed me you was my man, I was your girl
And I don't believe you doing laps and jump-and-jacks
    to go and see this other girl
I'm just not hearing it, when you tell me all of my love I have to stop
Because if I ain't got you now, then what the hell have I got
Tell me what does it mean,
    you're such the gentleman and opening doors
So what are you saying, the way it was, it still can't be that way no more
You had me easily, loved you completely, immediately it was so deeply
That I don't understand you now when you tell me that you don't need me

I don't get it,
    how you can even think you'd be better without me now
You had me so easily,

that you got me in such an angry space to listen to this right now
I loved you deeply,
	I was falling all the way to the bottom till there was none
What are you saying to me right now,
	after everything that we've done
I just don't get it,
	you played with me, all this love I had you took it away from me
Loved you completely,
	what didn't I do to make you wanna stay here with me
I loved you easily,
	I mean immediately I fell for you so deeply
That I don't understand it now when you tell me that you don't need me
	I don't get it…

AESSYNCE

WALK AWAY

You leave, you throw away everything and you leave, Thug you just leave
Then you let yourself be seen but you pretend you don't see me
I can't believe you talk that way, all of sudden so much to say
I can't believe you wanna go at it this hard this way,

      I can't believe the way you try to throw it back in my face
You had me spent, you had me went, you had me going and going
You had me sprung, you had me done, and I mean going and going
But you pull back every time, that same one move, that same one way
As soon as I let you back into my life again you only wanted to walk away

You leave, you go and give up on everything, you always leave
Then you show up here with another girl all over my territory
What the hell you doing here, after the day that you walked away
How the hell you have the nerve to show your face,

      and bring that buzzard around these ways
You had me spent, you had me went, you had me falling and falling
And I was feeling so good inside just by the way you was talking
But then you pull back every time, same one move, that same one way
As soon as I let you back into my life again you only wanted walk away

You leave, you just acted like it wasn't anything, Thug you just leave
Just act like it didn't matter, after you've been here with me
You leave, that same routine, always that same one way

As soon as I let you back into my life again you only wanted to walk away

And leave, listen to what everybody else say now, throw it all away

You had me, I mean you really really had me, thought you wanted to stay

But leave, you got that same one move, you go that same one way

Every time I let you back into my life again you only just walk away

You leave, you throw away everything and you leave, Thug you just leave

Then you let yourself be seen at the places that you see me

You leave...

AESSYNCE

FEELS LIKE

January 17, 2003

I don't know...

Looking at it sometimes, it don't feel right

When I apologize and I forgive you, then all we ever do is fight

It feels like you'll say anything 'cause you would do more than that to me

And tomorrow, more lonely than I can bear, I'll say baby come back to me

I don't know...

Stepping out and looking in, this ain't the same

When all I do is follow you but I'm the girl who takes the blame

It feels like, you'll take everything if I give to you, Mr. Pretty Damn Polite

But you'll call me a Ho and call me a Bitch

as soon as I do something else that you don't like. It feels like...

I don't know...

All this hassle for nothing, it don't seem worth it

'Cause all we do is ever argue about something that should be perfect

It feels like you'll do anything 'cause you could do more than that to me

And tomorrow more frantic than I can stand I'll say baby come back to me

I don't know...

Looking back in the mirror this can't be it

When all you do is cut me down and I pretend like I don't see it

It really feels like you'll do anything you can get away with,

Mr. SoPretty And DamnPolite

But you'll dog me out to everybody you think you can
　　　as soon as I do one more thing that you don't like

I stay up late, awake in bed, so many hours up every night
'Cause I don't know how the hell it feels so good
　　　if this is always the way it feels like
All this hassle for nothing, all this crying for nothing, I cry and cry
Because you'll always reach to put your hands on me
　　　when I say something that you don't like
　　　I don't know...
Looking at it sometimes, it don't feel right
When I apologize and I forgive you, then all we ever do is fight
It feels like you'll say anything 'cause you would do more than that to me
And tomorrow, more lonely than I can bear, I'll say baby come back to me
　　　I don't know...

A E S S Y N C E

HIDDEN AWAY

January 15, 2003

Looking for what you said was always there in the mirror and now I see
You can tell me that it ain't good enough and I'll do anything, I'm so sorry
In the end,

      I know it's nothing at all if you can't have it, gotta have your way
You wanna do what you wanna do but you won't meet me half of the way
I've tried to do things you wanted me to, I tried to see your point of view
I took the most horror I could from you, I did everything I could for you
A girl like me was bred of the bravest heart,

      in the roughest of times I chose to stay
Looking for what you said was so hard to find, was too far hidden away

I was looking for something that wasn't here before we met, but now I see
You tell me it ain't good enough and I'll keep on trying, I am so sorry
In the end,

      you're only getting to do all of the things you wanted to do with me
I'm taking you all the way when you're not doing anything to try and stay
I was trying to give it to you the way you wanted, afraid of not having you
But having you- was something that had never even mattered to you
A girl like me was bred of the bravest heart,

      in the roughest of times I chose to stay
Looking for what you said was so hard to find, was too far hidden away

Even if you wanted me it's too late,

    you lost me, now blame yourself

You wouldn't even expose yourself,

    so long I hoped you would let go of yourself

You don't embrace me for who I am,

    you want me to be what you want from me

You want me to go down all the way

    when you won't even commit enough and say you'll stay

I've tried to do things you wanted me to, I tried to see your point of view

I took the most horror I could from you, I did everything I could for you

A girl like me was bred to battle, in the roughest of times I chose to stay

Looking for what you said was so hard to find, was too far hidden away

I'm looking...

AESSYNCE

I REFUSE

January 14, 2003

You refused to give to me and offer me opportunities
So why am I hurting and hurting
    when you're not even falling in love with me
I gave you ample, I gave you more than enough, I don't have time
And I refuse to be stay with a man who just cannot make up his mind
You refused to put it out there, you didn't prove to me that this mattered
And I refuse to be that scene belonging to Bernadine
    hurting faster and faster

Me thinking back upon the days that I would try and you refused
Me thinking back about those other chicks-
    my name dragged throughout the dirt, my name abused
Me thinking about the way you take advantage of me-
    you used me all up now there ain't nothing else that you can use
So many times us working out was something you still refused

You refused to leave those be, was out here running these streets
So what other choice do I have left but to let you leave and do your thing
You refused to man up all the way,
    just refused to admit when your ass did wrong
And I don't wanna be talked about crazy no more,
    tell these nosy people to quit calling me on the telephone
I was suppose to be somebody, then I met you and then things changed

And I don't know who I am now,

      been too many clouds, been too much rain

Me thinking back upon the days that I would try and you couldn't choose
Me thinking back about those other chicks-

      my name dragged throughout the dirt for you, my shoes abused
Me thinking about the way you take advantage of me-

      you used me all up now I can't give you nothing else,

      it's nothing else you can use
So many times that us working out was something you would refuse

I tell the girls, this isn't what love is suppose to be doing to me
I kept trying to give it to him and he just kept refusing me
He refused, over and over I gave it to him to the maximum, he refused
I swear... over and over I tried to reach him and he didn't know what to do
He would refuse,

      this isn't what love is suppose to be feeling like all the time
I kept trying to make it work and he kept letting go all the time
He refused, he just kept walking out, I wasn't the one that he gave it to
I swear... over and over I tried to reach him and he didn't know what to do
He refused...

A E S S Y N C E

RAPING ME

January 13, 2003

It took my smile away, it took the light in my eyes away, it took my heart

It took my religion, it took my mind away, it took my spine, I'm torn apart

You walked away, you went to be with her, it took my spirit away from me

And every time I see you two together-

    it takes something away from me and it's raping me

It took my soul away, it took it's toll, it took all of my growth away

It took my words, it took my energy, it took my education and grades away

To think of where you move to put your hands on her,

    how can you ever reach to touch for me again

To think of the way you kissed on her,

    how can I ever believe a word you say again

It took my speech away, it took my sleep away, it took all of my appetite

It took my strength, being around new females, the girl won't be so nice

You cheated on me, you went with her, it took my dignity away from me

And every time I see you two together-

    it takes something inside away from me and it keeps raping me

Now when they see me, that girl so cool, it's a shame she ain't the same

I mean I love you but I'll never be able to be in love with you just the same

To think of where you move to put your hands on her,

    how can you ever reach to touch for me again

To think of the way you kissed on her,

    how can I ever believe a word you say again

How can I ever look into your eyes and see that man again,

      it took my vision, everything is different

How can I ever listen to you try to explain yourself when every word

      that comes from out of your mouth is disrespectful to women

How can I ever stand up and hold my head up high the same,

      when deep inside it took all of my pride away

And every time I think about you being with her and coming back to me,

      it's worse than murder, it's more than rape

It took my innocence away,

      now I'm just as hard as them other girls, to this I swear

I'm different, I'm just as cold blooded and disbelieving

      as all those other girls and I swear

To think of where you move to put your hands on her,

      how can you ever reach to touch for me again

To think of the way you kissed on her,

      how can I ever believe a word you say again-

      How can I trust you again?

A E S S Y N C E

Now Playing:

B 2 K

> I ' M   N O T   F I N I S H E D

these were all the words I *needed* to hear you say...

WITHOUT ME

January 12, 2003

My mind's emotionally distraught

I am mentally incapacitated, you infected my thoughts

Thinking of life without you now, hitting the panic to self-destruct

What could life be like without you now, I'm already corrupt

You don't know what you mean to me, this love has overloaded

Deeper than I ever was deep before, this is deep part 2, this is reloaded

My heart is dry,

      my eyes can't stand the sight to see you walking out on me

For loving you the best I could, how can you make it without me

Destroyed stability,

      in my bloodstream there's so much stress and so much pain

In anamnesis of your walking down these same hallways,

      all I ever see is rain

Ancient bows and powerful darts,

      but these weren't the arrows that cupid shot

You're not even the guy that I thought you were,

      this isn't the love that I first thought

Now I'm a wreck, I mean I use to try to do my best,

      I once kept myself up

But ever since I've been involved with you

      everything has tried to mess itself up

My heart is dry,

      my eyes can't stand the sight to see you walking out on me

For loving you the best I could,

      why would you win it without me

My mind is gone, the emotion has entered and overloaded

This is deeper than I ever was deep before, I promise you he reloaded

I'm so far out, I ain't got no remedy, my mind is so distraught

This is deeper than I ever was deep before, this man infected my thoughts

And now he thinks,

      I'm too damn crazy and he has to get rid of me while he can

And now he thinks he's better off, and that's the part I don't understand

I gave my heart till it was dry and now he's walking far out on me

Was loving him the best I could, how will he make it without me

Tell me how...

A E S S Y N C E

REMEMBER IT

January 11, 2003

I remember days you couldn't walk away
    and I couldn't leave from you either
Driving this thing on one accord,
    now we're just two different people
I'm just a girl and I'm not spoiled
    but I still love to have my way
And you still love to give it to me
    so why are we still acting this way
I remember days you had no patience for your friends
    to try to talk about me
This thing use to be just for you and me,
    but now we care about what everyone else may or may not think
Do you remember sitting across the room from me
    and wishing everyone else was gone
Could you try to remember there use to be times
    that it was so easy to get along

I remember a man who gave it to me my way,
    when my way was happening all the time
A man who chased me around in circles,
    and never thought that he was wasting his time
The man who wasn't so consumed with this hood life,
    remember that man so crystal clear

What happened to him,

    because he's not the same man who's standing here

I don't remember the wilding out,

    I don't remember no partying and late night boom boom rooms

And I don't remember you letting them boys try me

    like they could handle me the way you do

The man I loved with all my heart, do you remember,

    is he still there

The man who couldn't stand when we were apart,

    do you remember you use to care

You would never walk away,

    and I remember when nobody else knew your name

I'll be the first one to say it,

    you put on your thug costume and everything just changed

Do you remember sitting across the room from me

    and wishing everyone else was gone

Babe just try to remember...

    there use to be times that it was so easy to get along

The man I loved with all my heart, do you remember,

    is he still there

The man who couldn't stand when we were apart,

    do you remember you use to care

Remember me, remember you,

    remember everything that we've been through

Remember everything we use to be and everything I feel for you

    Remember...

A E S S Y N C E

AUGUST 22

January 11, 2003

You were meant to be my man and I was meant to be your girl
When God created deep love he brought the two of us in this world
I was meant to be your woman and you were meant to be my King
Because through loving you with every fiber inside of me,

      I become what it is to be a Queen
You were meant to be my husband and I was meant to be your wife
Because when He created happiness He put the both of us inside our lives
The vision was just of you, the solution was always you
Now everyday that I hold onto you, I see all of my dreams come true

August 22, 2001 was suppose to happen...
I didn't know how to wish but if I did it would be of you
God created the truth and I never felt a feeling such as this,

      but I always prayed for a man to be like you
You were meant to be the one and I was meant to be the only
When I tell you how much I love you, it's only for real and nothing phony
We were meant to be together, to ride and not let go
This bond we share so tight and this closeness we both know
The vision was just of you, the solution was always you
Now everyday that I hold onto you, I see all of my dreams come true
August 22, 2001 was suppose to happen...

AESSYNCE

...AND DEEPER

January 7, 2003

I'm deeper much deeper into this man King that you are

And I sink deeper and deeper into this love that breaks my heart

And I drown deeper and deeper in this erotic pool of you

And I fall deeper and deeper, I don't even know what to do with you

I go deeper much deeper into this burning of your flame

And I slip deeper and deeper every time that I hear your name

And I drop deeper and deeper still loving all of my thoughts of you

When I fall deeper and deeper remembering the first time I saw you

I'm dipping deeper and deeper

  into your fondness, you are fondness

I get deeper and deeper

  I can't keep calmness, nothing's beyond this

It's just deeper and deeper

  when I think of how much love you show for me

And I fall deeper and deeper

  remembering the first time you touched me

I swim deeper and deeper

  into your massive brute appeal

And I plunge deeper and deeper

  in these emotions you make me feel

As we coast deeper and deeper

       but then no time goes quite the same

And I fall deeper and deeper

       remembering the first time you called my name

I tub deeper and deeper when I feel you here next to me

I slither deeper and deeper towards your ray of light to a better she

And I flood deeper and deeper into those sweet dreams I have of you

And I fall deeper and deeper, every time that I come right back to you

As I think deeper much deeper, sometimes that I don't understand

I ponder deeper and deeper every time that I feel your hands

I wonder deeper more deeper than I had ever done before

As I fall deeper and deeper and then I thirst for this much more

I fall deeper and deeper...

A E S S Y N C E

INVISIBLE TEARS

January 6, 2003

These invisible virgin tears do fall from these virgin eyes
When you do those crazy things that really crush me inside
This girl that's so untouchable, you touched from underneath my clothes
That still sends these pulses through my hair down to the tip of my toes
You just don't see it,

    my education was not to be crying over these hood males
Because these boys they don't be caring and sensitive for these females
But these virgin tears do fall, from the bottom of my broken heart
And everybody has seen the most worst part,

    everybody knows who you are

Once silent screams inside my pillow and unseen tissue from unseen box
'Cause you can't see me crying, ever since I started I haven't stopped
I built a wall for my protection, but my armor is melting slow
My wall comes tumbling down and everything I thought I was right about

    I don't even know if it was even right no more
My education; what is meant to be will always find a way
'Cause a man who wanted love would've never lost it all and left this way
But still these virgin tears do fall, from the bottom of my broken heart
And everybody has seen the most worst part,

everybody knows who you are

These invisible virgin tears do fall from these virgin eyes...

And everybody has seen your face, everyone knows you're why...

AESSYNCE

CAN'T CHANGE

January 6, 2003

I can't change,

      I know it's been over a year but this is growth

And I didn't change,

      this is still River Road, this is the only thing I know

I said I'd never let you go,

      those words I spoke, I really meant it

I put my soul in it and when I opened my heart to you

      I promise you it was permanent

This is the testament, I can't change,

      ever since a year ago I've wanted to be with you

And I didn't change, I've never given up on the dream,

      I never lost the hope, I still see you

This is the same girl

      with the same heart with the same beat that beats for you

Boy, I could've left a long time ago if I wanted to,

      baby, I'm not leaving you

It's been too much of a struggle to stay two steps ahead of you,

      to stand here in front of you

But I didn't change,

      and I'll never take for granted all of the things I've done with you

You said goodbye,

      that stuff you did it made me cry, it's just the truth

Truth is, the same person I fell in love with

is the same person you decapitated,

     I can't regain that side of you

This is the testament I can't change,

     ever since one year ago I've been fighting and holding on

And I didn't change, I still have the same number

     if you wanna call me back on the telephone

I'm still the very same girl with the very same heart,

     with the very same beat that beats for you

Boy, I could've left a long time ago if I wanted to,

     I'm not leaving you

I can't change, come back to east Atlanta

     find me at South DeKalb Mall 'cause I didn't move

Come back to River Road, at Cedar Grove

     and I'll be waiting for you

I'll be saving my love for you,

     I'll lock it away and throw away the key

Because I can't change from loving you,

     so many times I said it, it wasn't true

I'm still the only one who can do things the way I do,

     can't nobody treat you the way I do

And I'm still doing all this for you,

     because of the deep deep love you made me do

I'm still the very same girl with the very same heart,

     with the very same beat that beats for you

Boy, I could've left a long time ago if I wanted to,

     baby, I'm not leaving you

I can't change...

A E S S Y N C E

JUST FRIENDS

January 5, 2003

Words between us that we both know won't go away
So silent could hear a pin drop but I just don't know which words to say
Is it a fact, is it a fiction, was it worth the risks and the mistakes
Because by now too much has happened to ever try to erase
It's so much tension, but in the end what is pure will still remain
No matter the desperate droughts, no matter the constant rain
You know I've tried to tell myself that we can never be more than friends
But every time I look inside your eyes boy I can never pretend

There are deep feeling's between us that we both know won't go away
So many times people told me to just get over it, told me it was just a faze
But you know that after me no girl will fill the role I made
I just wish I would've told you how I was deep in love with you everyday
Now that you're gone,
        when you look back, look in my heart, see your remains
When a girl like me really falls in love you know that love will never fade
'Cause I've tried to convince myself we can never be more than friends
But every time I look inside your eyes boy I can never pretend

We got feeling's between us, feeling's inside that ain't gon' change
No matter where you lay your hat, the home front's still the same
It doesn't matter where you go and it doesn't matter what you do
But who's gon' love you for the man you haven't even become yet,

       tell me who...

We got feelings between us, feeling's inside that just won't end

And every time I look into your eyes I'm not strong enough to pretend

I've tried to tell myself, I've tried to convince myself over and over again

Because every time I look into your eyes, I just don't wanna pretend

We can't be friends...

I don't wanna try to see you again...

If I can't be your girlfriend then I don't wanna just be your friend

We can't be friends...

I don't wanna run into your face again...

If I can't be your girlfriend then I don't wanna be colleagues then

We can't be friends...

I don't wanna fake, I just can't pretend...

Every time I look into your eyes I fall so deep in love again

We can't be friends...

I'm telling you I never wanna see your face again...

Every time I look into your eyes I fall so deep in love again

We can't be friends...

A E S S Y N C E

Now Playing:

Monica
>BEFORE YOU WALK OUT OF
MY LIFE

RIGHT HERE

What would I do if you were out of my life, what would I make of the day

When every time that I turn on the radio and the Monica song they play,

    all I do is see your face...

Without you here, I lay awake and I wait for you to reply

Black on my French tips, my gold lipstick,

    nothing I have worn has lasted as long as you and I...

And I've been thinking, I know you thought I wasn't ready before

Boy I ain't never been with anyone who ever treated me

    the way that you do me before...

And I'll be here, tattoo the Chevy symbol across my back, without all fear

Without compromise, without corruption, without disruption,

    I'll be right here

What would I do without you now, what would I do with lungs in me

'Cause if you leave there'd be no air, there'd be no water,

    there'd be no me

Without you here, I sit and wait for the mailman to pass this door

I never met a man who made me go so far

    and feel a love this deep before

And I've been thinking, what you mean to me, you mean this crazy world

Things have happened,

    but look at what's always been the very same, look at this girl

I've been right here, tattoo the Chevy symbol on my back, without all fear

Without compromise, without corruption, without disruption,

    I'll be right here

My white dress, the heart shaped locket across my chest,

    longer than that...

The scent of my perfume that filled this very room,

    my love goes stronger than that...

I'm going longer,

    longer than the 76er's vs the Laker's championship game...

And I'll be stronger,

    no matter what happens now I promise you I won't change...

But I've been thinking,

    what you mean to me, you mean this crazy world

Things have happened,

    but look at what's always remained real love, I'm still that girl

That's why I'm here, tattoo the Chevy symbol across my back,

    without all fear

Without compromise, without corruption, without disruption,

    I'm still right here

A E S S Y N C E

THE END

This can't be the end,

    there is no end, go to the edge of the earth and it still spins

This can't be done 'cause why does my heart still beat

    to your every footstep closer and closer then

You just can't leave, you won't be so cruel, you won't be so mean

And you're not gonna go be with her and we both lose everything

This can't be it, you just can't quit, it's so much love I have to bring

This can't be over, before I give up now I'll B.O.E on everything

You cannot do this, you cannot go be with her, beloved stay here with me

You're all I want, you're all I need, and I can't let you steal away from me

This can't be the end,

    there is no end, go to the lowest part of the stem and it still runs

This can't be done because why does my soul still feed

    from the fire in you just like the sun

You just can't go, you just can't be so bad, you can't be so stupid

And you're not gonna go be with her, and I'm not gonna let you do it

You just can't leave, I won't let you attempt it,

    I owe you something much more than you can afford

I'd rather suffer the hurt and pain,

    before I let you walk out and not come back no more

You cannot do it, you cannot be with her, beloved stay here with me

You're all I want, you're all I need and I can't let you steal away from me

This can't be the end...

A E S S Y N C E

-PART 2-

Drowning

From Aessynce

P.S. LOVE

The hardest thing ever was keeping everything inside. The joy. The pain. The love. And hate. It was like being imprisoned by my own happiness at times. Not being able to talk about us to anyone, even to those who already had their speculations. I mean, that part in itself was the heaviest for me. There was so much I wanted to express at times to friends and family but remained silent out of fear and obligation to you.

I'll never forget carrying that black journal to class every day, and verse-writing about everything that had taken place between us, no matter how small or how it made me feel. That little spiral tablet would become the escape for me. The small window of fresh air in a room with no doors and no vents. It gave me a voice. And every day I yelled my heart out inside of those pages. I screamed from the pit of my soul, and forced those words from deep inside of me that needed release. In the end, weights would be lifted from my shoulders and the pressure would eventually die away.

I realized how much strength it had taken from me to hide and cover up these emotions I felt for you all of those months, only when I had no more energy left. And it wasn't just from the world I was protecting it from, but often times even you. There were things I never wanted to say because I wasn't as confidant enough and I couldn't say. There were times I just wasn't willing to submit my pride to give you another chance to break my heart any further. I couldn't take anymore rejection. And for that I do apologize. For all the love I have for you, I owed it to you one last time to forgive you. To trust you. To believe in you. And I do!

NEVER KNEW

December 30, 2002

introduction spoken by J E W E L:

> Emotions evoked through pain
>
> Sadness of softest rains, love maintained
>
> Broken and given back but never like new
>
> Tarnished and tainted heart, a young girl dressed in blue

A E S S Y N C E speaks:

You never opened your eyes,

> so long I've tried to make you see it but you didn't never

So fortunate you could've been, but you let it get blown away

> far in the wind, and now we can't be together

You never looked long enough to see me still standing here,

> I was deep in love with you

Thinking I wouldn't stick by you and ride for you

> you should've known it wasn't true

You never looked hard enough,

> many men would've realized this girl is solid

But by you this girl was gotten,

> but it's too bad you never saw it

You never knew how much I loved you too,

> so much I've tried to make you see my love was you

You never opened your eyes to finally realize,

> what I wanted in my life was a guy like you

You never opened your mind,

> so long I've wanted to let you in and rush to show you more

And I put it out there so many times,

> but it was just rejected before

You never thought long enough,

> a girl like me was wifey material, a girl like me is pure

So many times I let you look into my eyes,

> but you could never be sure

You never thought hard enough, you never put your faith in me,

> let those envious turn you away from me, you didn't know better

And I've seen you with some new girl now

> is that the reason why we couldn't be together

You never knew how much I loved you too,

> so much I've tried to make you see my love was you

But you never opened your eyes to finally realize,

> what I was missing in my life was a guy like you,

You never knew...

outro spoken by J E W E L:

> Love was taken, love rejected then given back
>
> The last resort again... Dangerously Deep again

A E S S Y N C E's dedication

Jewel, I thank you for being part of this and giving yourself so freely. Our friendship through these hard times really helped me to pull through a lot. I wish you nothing but happiness and success. Mwah! DIVA ☺

A E S S Y N C E

Now Playing:

Mary JBlige

>I LOVE YOU

IN FRONT

December 28, 2002

Even if I closed my eyes it would be too late, I already saw the truth
Even if I walked away, you had your hands in the cookie jar and I saw you
Your hands were, your lips were too, I saw you kiss her in the face
And I can't lie, before we met,

  I'd never be standing here looking stupid as hell this way

Seeing her arms around you now, looking in your eyes, embrace so tight
Touching her, your hands all over her, must've been hard to say goodbye
'Cause you're so good to her, you're too good for her,

  that's good for her and not for me

To see you dating a brand new girl

  standing right here in front of me

Even if I turned around and left right now, it'd be too late, boy it's no lie
I saw you looking into her eyes,

  while people stood around checking for the both of you guys

With your body on her, I had to fight the tears it made me cry
If you were trying to make me jealous I swear

  I could've just fell to the floor and covered my face to hide

Seeing you kiss like it was Valentines, your affections to her so sweet
And your hands around her waist, it must've been so hard to leave
'Cause you're so good to her, you're too good for her,

  how good for her and not for me

To see you dating a brand new girl standing right here in front of me

Even if you lied and told me she was just a friend,
      I saw the truth
Even if she lied and told me too,
      I already caught you and I saw you
So many times I let you tell me I couldn't handle
      having a hood thug just like you
But if you were in my shoes with a man like you,
      you would've left a long time ago, wouldn't you...
Seeing your eyes on her right now, you looked at all those other girls
Those easy girls, those gullible girls, you had your body on all those girls
Being good for her, so good to her, only for them and not for me
To see you dating these brand new girls
      standing right here in front of me
I see...

A E S S Y N C E

FOR ETERNITY

Fingertips...

    running through every beautiful strand of your afro hair

Hands...

    gripping the back of your neck, attar you sprayed right there

Arms...

    around your shoulders, dawning my femininity

Heart...

    is going long with everything that God put into me

Chest...

    against your lungs, your ribs, I'll never leave

Back,

    on all those doubters, all I hear are love's sweet harmonies

Boy all this love is for eternity,

    no matter the direction of your 54'11 shoes

This love will last eternity,

    that I'll be right here -in here- with you

Body,

    wanted for nothing until the day I knew your name

Mind,

    everything I didn't know about you never made the feeling change

Feet,

    on the ground with every step, history is what we've made

Soul,

      is on a joyride, I don't wanna take it slower and slower each day

Lips,

      the sweetest virgin kiss, no love in front of you

Eyes,

      don't see nobody else, no man I want but you

This love is for eternity,

      no matter the direction of your 54'11 shoes

This love will last eternity,

      that I'll be right here -in here- with you

Eternally,

      and I mean never, I will never stop being true

And the way you looked back at me in my eyes,

      I knew you would feel the same way that I do

Eternally, and I mean only one,

      because to what we've become I wasn't blind

And I felt it before I said it,

      it's been inside of me even before all of this encountered time

Eternally,

      and I mean really loving you is the thing that I will do

And I mean never tell a lie,

      I will never stop being true

Eternally...

...

This love will last eternity, that I'll be right here -in here- with you...

AESSYNCE

REMEMBER ONCE

December 21, 2002

I remember the first time I saw you, I will never forget the day
Like no matter how far we go I will never forget your face
And I remember the day you touched me, the first time I felt your hands
And I felt something ignite inside that told me, one day he'll be my man
The day that you called my house,
     I must've jumped on the bed a hundred times
Thirty-four, Thirty-four, Seven hundred and seventy-eight,
     by the of the day I had that number all the way down memorized
But now it's different, but I remember the time we use to take
Once upon a time when we were good it never use to be this way

I remember the first time and every time I looked inside of your eyes
And I felt trembles deep down inside that said, one day he's gon' be mine
And I remember the first day of our 10th grade, I was cute, I was intelligent
There were so many times I wanted to stand up and introduce myself,
     hi my name is Aessynce…
Now those days are far away, so crazy how things just changed
In the beginning you'd never cuss at me and never call me out my name
Like now you do, but I remember the reverence we use to have
Once upon a time we were good and even the bad times weren't so bad

I remember the fights we use to drag out and have it,
     I'd say I won

You'd say you won,

    we'd make a mess and look at the craziness we'd both done

I forgave you when I hated to,

    who were you to do those crazy things to me

And who was I to even let you,

    what the hell was I really thinking

I remember the first time I caught you with a chick,

    you said this girl just came along

And then was another one and another one,

    and then another skank came along

I kid you not,

    remember nobody could tell me nothing bad about you

'Cause your feeling's for me had showed,

    and everything in this world I had was you...

Now all I do is remember,

    when you use to be you, remember I use to be me

Now all I seem to think about is when we use to try to be the couple

    I always hoped we'd be

I still remember,

    the 112 song they played on the radio the day you left

And all I seem to think about is when we met,

    I was so shy and I was so scared to just be myself

The day that you called my house,

    I must've jumped on the bed a hundred times

Thirty-four, Thirty-four, Seven hundred and seventy-eight,

    by the of the day I had that number all the way down memorized

But now it's different,

but I remember the time we use to take

Once upon a time when we were good and it never use to be this way

I remember…

A E S S Y N C E

POEM CRY

December 19, 2002

I dangerously love you, these are bottomless tears

We got connections, we got ties that I feel deep down all the way in here

Deeper than rivers, it only started out as a pond now this is plentiful

My womanly love crashes into your manly pride,

     now the both of us are electrified

Drip- Drip… Drop- Drop…

     I just wanted this pain to stop

I just want your kisses in place of everything

     when we both said what we didn't mean a lot

Because this cloud's still hanging 'round, the winds still in my eye

And I can't see pass this anymore, all I do is cry… cry…

Lord I've been weaken down to both of my knees

This is something stronger than just two 15yr olds,

     even the bold and beauty queens

It's wider than oceans, bigger than the Titanic,

     more necessary than paddles

Going back and forth,

     loving you is worth the life of the battle

Drip- Drip… Drop- Drop…

     I just can't stop these tears that fall

I just wish we could go back and what went wrong,

we could try to just fix it all

Because this cloud's still hanging 'round, the winds still in my eye

And I don't see pass this anymore, and all I do is cry… cry…

A year I wanted you, one year I needed you

I cried for fifteen months I wasted to try to be with you

I cried these sixty weeks, it was easy to hurt and harder to walk away

Because I cried every one of four hundred, seventy-five days

     that you threw away and you just washed down the drain

Fifty thousand, nine hundred and sixty-eight hours

     thinking my world would come to end

And I cried three million, fifty-eight thousand and eighty minutes

     waiting for you to come back and cheat again

I cried eighteen million, three hundred and forty-eight thousand,

     four hundred and eighty seconds I use to think I'd die

And this cloud's still hanging 'round, baby all I do is cry…

     cry…

AESSYNCE

LAST BREATH

December 18, 2002

To Mr. Dangerously Deep, this is to you babe…

My heart is dying, I've been trying and trying, this is the truth

All night I've just been crying and crying,

      with the "Thug left and gone away for good" blues

You gotta know, after this long row I never wanted to see you go

Didn't wanna give up yet,

      I didn't think it was over the day that you told me so

Deep down I wanna keep on trying and keep on caring

Deep down I wanna keep on fighting and keep on daring

It's me still around and I'm still swinging, I still got a lot of love in me left

And I'm still kicking, and I'm still here down to the very last breath

My soul is crying, I've been trying and trying, my heart's been broke

My love's been hurt, trying to keep it from dying and not let go

Not for another woman situation, not for another girl to steal you now

Not for another man to come along and take me far away from you now

Deep down I wanna keep on waiting and keep on hoping

Deep down I wanna keep on staying and keep on working

It's me still around and I'm still wishing, I still got a lot of love in me left

That's why I'm still hanging on and loving strong until the very last breath

I won't exhale until it's over, you might as well suffocate me in your arms

'Cause I won't breathe until you see with me is where you belong

I will not kiss, I will not hug, I will not touch, I will not feel
I just won't exist until we exist and I gotta keep faith one day we will
Deep down I wanna keep on praying and keep believing
Deep down I wanna keep on struggling and keep on speaking
It's me still around and I'm still screaming, I still got a lot of love in me left
And I'm still kicking, I'm still here with you down till the very last breath
I said I'm here...

AESSYNCE

Now Playing:

Sade

>NO ORDINARY LOVE

BE YOURS

December 18, 2002

I'm breathing to be, dreaming to be, faithfully I'm living to be your one

Your one woman, the only woman you wanted, I'm wanting to be that one

I'm wishing to be, picturing,

     so much I'm listening to be the only one you call

In the morning, in the high of afternoon, in the midnight hour,

     I just wanna be the one woman that you can call

I'm hoping to be, showing you I can be, I'm growing to be your love

Your unwavering love, your honest love, committed love, I feel deep love

I've been longing inside to set free, I've been honing inside of me,

     it's been so buried alive in me

For you to spend these times with me,

     over the edge that it's driving me

I'm waiting to be, craving to be, crazy to be your new leaf

I am humming, sitting here wondering, about all of the feasibility's

I stayed to be as patiently, I've been the peaches and I've been cream

And together we'll overcome these hurdles that lie in front of us,

     and at last we'll outrun everything

I'm hoping to be, sowing to be, I'm glowing to be your love

Your real love, your toughest love, committed love, I feel deep love

I've been longing inside to just set free, I've been honing inside of me, it's been so buried alive in me

For you to spend these times with me,

over the edge that it's been driving me, I desire to be...

A E S S Y N C E

NO MORE

December 14, 2002

When I fell in love with you, you became for me disinterested

I gave you what you was chasing for and everything became so different

You didn't want for me no more, you wasn't deep for me no more

When the chase was there no more, you just didn't need me anymore

When I grew to care as much as you cared about what happened to me

When I liked it just as much as you liked the day that you said
>   you first saw me

When I fell deep, forthwith all of my emotions you just ignored

When your curiosity was there no more,
>   you didn't feel love for me no more

When I was starting to love, you started pushing it back, you pulled away

You just stopped caring, you didn't give a damn if I left here or if I stayed

You didn't wanna talk to me no more,
>   you didn't wanna speak to me no more

Like the fun was all over now, you didn't wanna see me here no more

Your thrill was then fulfilled, it was your time to move on

Once you knew that you could have me you just left me alone

When I fell dangerously deep with you, forthwith I got ignored

The attraction was then no longer and you didn't want for me no more

Because you only wanted for me when I didn't never want you back

And you only called me first when I didn't wanna call you back

You only wanted for me at first 'cause you didn't know I wanted you

And just because you walked away it's not that simple for me to do

Like after you knew that you could have me

      you didn't wanna come back to me

And once you knew how you could get to me,

      you didn't feel bad about if you were missing me

Once I fell dangerously deep for you,

      you wanted to open the door and not come back no more

And when you knew I loved you too,

      for you it wasn't as deep no more…

A E S S Y N C E

I PROMISE

December 13, 2002

I promise you love, I promise to you all my love, here's all my love

For the rest of my life I'll be ever deeply, ever dangerously in love

So many nights alone in my bed I only wanted to be with you

Sleep with you, breathe with you, I just wanted to be with you

You gotta know, it's nothing like it, December just gets so cold

And I've been loving you all this time and I just want you to know

Sexy lips is my signature, nights in the mirror I practiced to get it right

To get you back into my life I promise to make it right

I'll do it, I'll ride you up and I'll go down the highest elevator

I'll do it, tonight I'm gon' get on my baddest behavior

I promise, I promise to you all the life, this is my life

I promise to you the woman that I'll be later on, I wanna be in your life

It's gon' be good, it's gon' be worth the wait, it's gon' be worth your while

It's gon' be something to talk about, it's gon' be worth your every dial

I promise, nothing is gon' feel like the time we spend together

You don't need to worry about them other chicks,

    I got something that's gon' be better

Sexy lips is my signature, nights in the mirror I practiced to get it right

To get you back into my life I promise to make it right

I'll do it, I'll ride you up and I'll go down the highest elevator
I'll do it, tonight I'm gon' get on my super baddest behavior

A E S S Y N C E

IN LOVE

December 8, 2002

Xscape, we are alone and I'm playing this song for you
Practiced the lines a million times and for nobody but you
Let the spotlight be one on you and let the spotlight shine one on me
Let it happen, it's taking place, the words are coming right out of me
No dilemma's, escaping the negative, you belong here in my life
It's been some times things wasn't right but the love we just can't fight
Don't do me wrong, don't treat me bad, I'm giving you all my love
Just don't break my virgin heart, how much I feel, this is deeply in love

I don't wanna escape, with you is where I find my heart, I find my soul
Waited so long to be here now and I don't wanna let go
Tighter and tighter, squeeze me tighter and tighter, it's now in play
Take it all the way down and lose control, I just don't wanna escape
Don't walk away it's so much between us now that everything must be true
So much that we've been through
        has only made me feel that much more so close to you
Don't do me wrong, don't treat me bad, I'm giving you all my love
Don't you break my virgin heart, how I feel, this is being deeply in love

        Don't you do it,
nothing I own is worth more than doing it, we've pass the bar
Nothing I own is worth more than the two people together that we both are
In it, I've fallen, I've been falling and falling I can't escape

I'm your girl and you're my baby, to forget you now would be too crazy
I can't escape it, I don't wanna get off the dream ride that this is
We've come such a long ways from the beginning,

      I don't remember feeling like this
Don't do me wrong, don't treat me bad, I'm giving you all my love
Don't you break my virgin heart, the way I feel, this is being deeply in love
The way I feel...

A E S S Y N C E

ALL ALONE

December 6, 2002

Puzzled, it just doesn't fit, look at the colors

Look at the picture, these two people don't show love to each other

Look at the lines, everybody's crossing the line, look at the edge

This is a maze, these people have no life in the eyes, they look so dead

Is it me, it's gotta be more to it, this can't be me

Is this the way that it really looks but I've been too stupid to try to see

Is it really a trap, look at the picture, is all hope really gone

What have I been waiting for all this long...

    Why am I standing here all alone...

It just ain't right, look me in my face, tell me this can't be right

Look at this picture, all these tears, look at what you've done to all my life

Feels like I'm stuck inside a hallway with no windows and no doors

Feels like I'm trapped inside a puzzle and I can't figure this out no more

Is it me, is it suppose to be love, it don't seem fair

Is it suppose to be fussing and calling names,

    is it suppose to be anger there

Am I stuck inside a trap, look, is all hope really gone

What have I been waiting for all this long...

    Why am I standing here all alone

What is this puzzle, what is this maze, what's forcing these raging colors

Look at the picture, look at the pain, we don't show love to each other

Why am I sitting here by this phone when you ain't never gonna call

And why am I willing to give it up, why am I waiting to risk it all

I think it's a trap,

you'll let me close enough to only slam the door in my face so hard

Is it suppose to still hurt, you'll let me in deep enough before you leave

      and break my heart

It was only a trap, look at it now, all hope's really gone

What have I been waiting for all this long...

      Why am I standing here all alone...

      I tell myself, "Girl just stay strong..."

A E S S Y N C E

YOU'RE HAPPY

I tried, but we both know no matter what that something's there
And I pretend, I so pretended, if you didn't care then I didn't care
The day I saw you with another girl it really opened my eyes to see
All those things you do for her you never wanted to do for me
I acted, I was an actress, if you didn't want this, I didn't want you
'Cause you was fronting like you didn't want everything that I wanted too
There was no girl here, no girl on earth, who could've felt as sad as me
To know that she's the one that you really love,

    she's the one who makes you happy

I performed, gave the performance of my career, I will survive
I operated, smooth operator, but that knife really hurt inside
I ignored it long as I could, how the hell you're out here doing it for this girl
And for me, you didn't never do nothing,

    tell me who is this high school girl
Because I tried, Heaven knows, I'm not as hard as you, I tried to leave
But every time I think about seeing that other chick,

    my heart just gets the best of me
There was no girl here, no girl on earth, who could've felt as sad as me
To know that she's the one that you really love,

    she's the one who makes you happy

I've struggled, it's been a struggle to eat, struggle to sleep

I've been faking, because this smile in the hallway, that's just not me

I'm hurting so bad, I never thought that you would do this to me

Because how much you love that girl you really proved it to me

Holding hands, kissing in front of everybody, now you're Mr. Popularity

And where I was lost before, I've found it now, and I see clarity

No girl here, no girl on earth, who could've felt as sad as me

To know that she's the one that you really love,

    she's the one who makes you happy

I tried...

AESSYNCE

IT HURTS

December 5, 2002

When I want you more than life and I can feel it so deep
With a passion and desire even stronger than me
When I need you more than I can resist, more than everything I see
When I just can't control myself and I have to cry myself to sleep
When it hurts so deep, it hurts so bad, you gotta know that it hurts
And I feel pain that's so insane every time that I hear your name
When my heart's broken to pieces and you are all I ever had
Just when I think I can't take no more, every time that it hurts so bad

I want you and you don't understand what it all is doing to me
It's everything and that emotion is even more frightening and confusing
      than it is to you right here for me
When I love you more than I want to, than I need to, when I see you
With a fire in my soul and I just need to when I need you
It hurts so deep and I can't talk about it 'cause people won't understand
How you didn't never ask me to be your girl,
      but I'm still calling you as my man
When my world is torn in two and you are everything left I have
Just when I think I can't take no more, every time that it hurts so deep
So bad…

AESSYNCE

Now Playing:

Toni Braxton

>SEVEN WHOLE DAYS

JUST TIRED

December 3, 2002

Tired of waiting on your heart to know if you even love me or not

Tired of not liking what's in the mirror, I am a leopard, yes I have spots

Tired of guessing if you just broke up with me or not, love should be bliss

From the start of this I put my heart in this

      but real love shouldn't be like this

Just tired of waiting, I'm tired of waiting for the 15 candles and 15 roses

The 15 minutes of you just looking at me and kissing my lips the slowest

I'm tired of waiting for this everyday rain to stop anticipating your rescue

I'm tired of waiting and I can't take it,

      this constant indecision boy I can't take it...

I'm tired of waiting to be the girl inside of your black and orange

      leather New York 76ers jacket

Tired of holding back my love so deep out of fear

      that you'll just say I'm overreacting

Tired of guessing if every time you leave will you come back or not,

      love should be bliss

So many times I slammed the door and I walked away

      I just really hate doing this same old sh--

I'm tired of waiting for when all this just gon get better

      and be the way it's suppose to be

And not telling you how much I love you

'cause you never say that you're in love with me
I'm tired of waiting for this everyday rain to stop
    anticipating your rescue
I'm tired of waiting and I can't take it,
    this constant indecision boy I can't take it...

I'm tired of waiting...
    so you might as well leave and don't you ever come back
All this time that you was around here,
    as if you were something much more than all of that
I'm tired of going, boy I declare, real love should be as bliss
And when I see those happy people, their love don't look like this
Just tired of waiting on your heart to know if you ever loved me or not
Tired of not liking what's in the mirror, yes I am leopard, I still have spots
I'm tired of guessing if every time you leave will you come back or not,
    love should be bliss
So many times I slammed the door and I walked away,
    and I'm tired of doing this same old sh--
I'm tired of this...

A E S S Y N C E

SHARE TOGETHER

December 2, 2002

After the rain the sun will come out to shine again,

    there'll be more days to come

There'll be more clouds ahead

    but there's too many good times forth us to come

Don't even think it, don't you try it,

    we've got bigger things to make it through

So don't you ever try to tell me,

    that this is too much to suck up and do

The flowers will bloom again,

    the roses will grow once more

And everything that led us down to this very moment

    will be irrelevant going forth

Even after these words are over, I promise when this world's over

We'll be there together, we'll be paired together, we will share it together

Can't stand still, the herd will move again, the climate will change again

We gotta pull this thing together before the machines come back again

Don't you think it, Don't you do it, look this way, don't disregard

Don't you ever leave this love behind for wolves to tear it apart

Don't you forget, the feast will happen, the harvest will come again

Don't give up on what's in stored for us, the promise will never end

Even after this poem is over, I swear when this earth is over

We'll be there together, we'll be paired together, we will share it together

This is worth everything, more than breathing, more than sleeping,
    I believe it
And I'd push every woman off this damn planet,
    if you could open your eyes and try to see it
Even after the mic goes out,
    when all the city lights die out
Even after the road burns out
    and the emergency lines run out
We'll be strong together, we'll hold on together,
    we will belong together
We'll be there together, we'll be paired together,
    we will share it together
After the rain, the sun will shine again, there will be more days to come
And there will be more clouds ahead,
    but there's still so many good times forth us to come-
    After the rain...

AESSYNCE

200 WORDS

December 1, 2002

These are my two hundred words...

He is Chicago, he's unexplored by me,

he's something new to me, he is this unspoiled life

He is strength and he is physical,

he is this day, he is this night

He is every man wrapped into one,

he is the good, he is the bad

He's fascination, he is fixation,

and I feel temptation I never had

He's the feeling like when you put on a pair of shoes

that's killing the outfit girls just would hate on

He is gravity, he's enormity,

he's the energy I can't seem to push away from

He's the past behind my lady-hood,

the future in front of my womanhood

The purpose, he is reason,

and he's got just a big enough bag of manhood

He is the answer, he is Sagittarius,

he is super, he is star

He is spirit and he is fire,

he is the essence of what is heart

He is so much time, he is emotion,

he is everything to me and everything to do

And before I leave something important out

if you believe in nothing else, just know this much is true

I'll love you for the rest of my life, I swear to you...

And these are the 200 hundred words I sat up all night

and tried to write about you-

Dedicated to you...

AESSYNCE

KISS ME

November 30, 2002

I like... a bad boy, I like... those v-neck tees

I like the way you walk when you wear your jeans

      every time you walk over to talk to me

I like... a bad boy, I like... how you addressing me

I like the way you try not to smile but you can't help it

      every time you come next to me

Closer and closer you come, deeper and deeper I always slip

I've been waiting until I met the right guy

      and now I think that this could be it

I like... a bad boy, I like... your mustache shape

I like the way you walk in the room

      and all the other girls turn to look this way

I like... a big... boy... I like a man who's running sh--

I like the way you check my attitude

      every time that I'm talking it

I like... a big... boy... I like a man with hands like you

I like that look in your eyes when you stare at me,

      I swear I've always wanted a man like you

Closer and closer you try to come, deeper and deeper I only slip

I've been waiting until I found just the right guy

      but now I think that this could be it

I like... a big... boy... I like the tone of your arms

And I like the way I feel when you come closer

      I wanna ring the alarms

Kiss me... 'cause I can't wait and I really like...

Over and over what I think of you every time that I fantasize

You bad boy, I really do, you sexy boy I really like those v-neck tees

I like the way you walk when you wear your jeans

      every time you walk over to talk to me

Kiss me... and I can't wait I really like...

Over and over what I know about you every time that I fantasize

A big... boy, I like a man with hands so big just like you

I like that look in your eyes when you stare at me,

      I swear I've always wanted a man like you

      And I can't wait...

A E S S Y N C E

SEXY, BEAUTIFUL

November 27, 2002

The deepest, sexiest, beautiful love...
I'm calling for you, my body calls all day and night
And if loving you is unfavorable,
I'm sorry I won't apologize for the rest of my life
  The deepest, sexiest, beautiful love...
I'm waiting, my body has waited these hours slow
And when you walk into this room,
I'll show you everything that you want me to show
  To deepest, sexiest, beautiful love...
Get me, I can't wait for you to get me and not let go
And faster,
I just wanna go faster and lose control
As soon as you get here, as soon as I see you,
every second I'm gonna give it away
All surrounding figures they fade away-
  behind this sexy beautiful love

How I feel, inside my body is heat, it's massive heat
And when I hear those footsteps up those stairs
I know you're coming for me
  The deepest, sexiest, beautiful love...
Against the wall, all over the carpet and closet too

Get me, I can't wait for you to get me all over this freakin' room

To deepest, sexiest, beautiful love...

I've been holding back until I knew

But this is a drug and I'm addicted, and the high is all for you

As soon as you get here, as soon as I see you,

every minute I'm gonna give it away

All surrounding figures they fade away-

behind this sexy beautiful love

They fade away...

AESSYNCE

FIRST TIME

November 24, 2002

You swept me off of my feet,
    I never knew how deep I fell when I fell down
I never knew how much I needed love until you wasn't around
I was fourteen, I was fifteen, I was still so timid and so naïve
In and out, inside and out of me, I let you run, I let you leave
You slowly became too comfortable, had to have these things your way
Doing what you did best the most, you pushed my feelings away
And the first time, I told you once you won't raise your voice
    when you talk to me, you look so stunned
The first time I told you I won't tell you no more you won't
    call me out of my name like the past times you have done

    I swear...
You swept me off of my feet, I never knew how hard I fell when I fell down
I never knew how far I had to go until you wasn't around
Fifteen, that's why I was silent, I wasn't as confident, I always took it
But I know if the roles were different,
    you couldn't handle this and you wouldn't
All this time you got so comfortable, I use to relapse to see you go
I bet you never thought you'd see the day that I'd stand up and tell you no
Because the first time, I say it's Aessynce, you can call me nothing less
Is the first time you made it clear,
    maybe I should go be with somebody else

Your swept me off of my feet,

      looking for you now 'cause you don't wanna come around

Because the first time I stood up

      was just like never laying down

So arrogant you become,

      looking for you now, you can't be found

Because the first time I draw the line you shouldn't have crossed,

      it was just like never staying down

And the first time, I told you once, you won't raise your voice

      when you talk to me, you look so stunned

The first time I told you I won't tell you no more, you won't

      call me out of my name like the past times you have done

Your chest stuck out, like I would owe you something,

      now you don't wanna be around

Because the first time that I stood up was just like never laying down...

      Fifteen.

AESSYNCE

I AM

November 23, 2002

Violated I am, nothing in this world could be nothing to take your place
And no matter what happens now, I'm still gon' love you anyway
Annihilated I am, when I turn around and look back, I don't see you
And to get you back behind me now, ain't nothing that I wouldn't do
Smashed to pieces,
      I see only the smoke ahead, the horn's have turned to silence
It's an emergency,
      what happened to all the flashing lights, Lord where are the sirens
The chandeliers, the shiny bracelets, the vintage rings across my hands
Violated I am, annihilated, I have nothing I am

Demolished to pieces, I am crippled, I have no fingers, I can not signal
I am immobilized, I'm paralyzed, I cannot operate in my own vehicle
Violated is what I am, I don't know where the hell this is, I have no map
How much deeper can I travel?
      I don't know how much further my love can last?
I don't have nothing that matter's here,
      rich girls and beauty queens don't matter here
I was never so superficial, but material things just do not matter here
The big purses, the matching heels, the vintage rings across my hands
Annihilated I am, I don't have nothing, I am nothing I am

My life ain't life, if my life can't be inside of your life, nothing I am

On earth, it has no worth if I'm not her- baby nothing I am

And breath is breath 'cause I'll be dead, smashed to pieces is what I am

'Cause I won't do this life thing, without you cannot be the right thing,

      violated is what I am...

My world just ain't a world if I ain't your girl, baby nothing I am

And I might be foolish but I've tried and I cannot do this, nothing I am

Without the jeans, without the hair, without the ring still on my hand

I'll be nobody, annihilated, I'll be nothing I am

I am...

                  A E S S Y N C E

DEFINING "DEEPER-NESS"

November 22, 2002

There was always a deeper part of me,
     then you created this deeper-ness
Deep into my virgin heart, deep in my soul,
     into my being this
All my love comes down,
     deep in chest, deep in my veins, deep in my blood
After the rain, after it floods,
     this is still the testament, God created love
So you'd have to get a shovel,
     you would have to dig a hole and keep on digging
You would have to climb in and keep on shoveling
     till you get to the ending
And that's where I'll be,
     that's where the fire will be and that is where it'll stay
Deep in the bottom, deep in the burrow,
     where nobody gets in the way

I've seen the day but you took all of the clouds away,
     now it's sunshine
Everywhere I go, everywhere I turn,
     I got my shades on all the time
There was always that peach tree that stood so tall
     they could never hack down
It was just like us the roots grew long,

the roots grew strong beneath the ground
That's why you'd have to get a shovel,
and you would have to dig a tunnel and keep on digging
You would have to climb in and keep on tunneling
till you get to the ending
And that's where I'll be, that's where the fire will be,
and that is where it'll stay
Deep in the bottom, deep in the burrow,
where no one else stands in the way

There was always a deeper part to me,
then you created this deeper-ness
Deeper than what my brain could know,
and I just can't believe I'm seeing this
The strongest parts about me are because of you,
you dug and you made me deep
Now I've turned into so much woman
I never thought I could be
So you would have to get a hoe,
and you would have to dig a hole and keep on digging
You would have to crawl in and excavate
until you get to the ending
And that's where I'll be, that's where the fire will be
and that is where it will stay
Deep in the bottom, deep in the pit,
where the world can't get in the way
That's where I'll be...

AESSYNCE

SISTER POEMS

November 19, 2002

I have to thank my younger sister Jean for sharing this piece with me…
Thank you for believing and being part of my dream. Let's do it!

JEAN speaks:

If I gave to you the world with a Blue Jay in the sky
If I gave you a fist of gold with all that money can buy
If I gave to you the stars with all the joy in the world
Would you see me, would you call me, would I always be your girl
If I gave to you a hug, no if I gave you a cheek, would you kiss it
If I read you a poem like this would you find the heart to listen

AESSYNCE speaks:

If I gave to you my heart, would you trust me,
    a girl like me will never stray
If I gave you a miracle,
    would you let me in and take all your inhibitions away
If I gave you the softest touch, the sweetest kiss,
    would you cherish the day
Would you breakdown on bended knee,
    and let love guide your heart down every step of the way
Would you promise to be around, if I promised to pledge my all
I got a lot of love to give if you tell me it's safe to fall

J E A N and A E S S Y N C E speak:

If I opened up my heart to you/

> and gave you every little bit that I had inside

Would it be enough to make you love me/

> would you never leave from by my side

If I let it all out to you/

> and I believed in me and you

Would you promise to me the truth/

> and say those words I love you too

If I gave to you an ocean/

> if I gave to you a tide

If I gave to you a rock of gold/

> would you give me the hope inside

If I gave to you my arms/

> when I was gone would you miss it

If I gave to you a poem like this/

> would you promise me you would listen

If I...

A E S S Y N C E

Now Playing:

Brandy

>ANGEL IN DISGUISE
>HAVE YOU EVER

GRAVY IS

November 18, 2002

From this hatred I wanna shield you,
    inside this fortress I will build you
Inside my love, inside my heart, inside these arms,
    here I'll conceal you
I'm just me,
    those pretty girls ain't all what they appear to you
So many females acted one way but I'm always gon' be the same way,
    and I wanna make it crystal clear to you
From this world I will protect you,
    at the forefront standing next to you
Through perils and testimonials,
    I will stand trial every test with you
I wanna make sure nothing bad is gonna happen,
    I just want you to be happy
As you're falling asleep in front of me,
    gravy is everything I want it to be

I wanna keep you safe, from harm I'll keep you away,
    your secret place
Inside my love, inside my open arms,
    I wanna be your getaway
Your girl is real, and I don't listen to what people think,
    and I can't listen to what everybody tells me that they know

Because I know you better than anyone else's word,

    and I know for you the world has been so cold

I still remember the day that I first saw your face,

    and it was so wonderful to finally meet

That's why from yourself I wanna teach you,

    from these other girls I wanna keep

They don't wanna make sure that nothing bad is gonna happen,

    they don't wanna make you as happy

But while you're falling asleep in front of me,

    gravy is all I ever want everything for you to be

Watching you sleep,

    I see a man so perfect and I don't want no one to hurt it

I won't let no one destroy it because I need it,

    even you gotta know it

When I watch you sleep,

    I want nothing for me 'cause I want everything for you

'Cause I can't be selfish, love is giving,

    and I'll give anything you need me to

Your girl is hood, I fight for you,

    I've dedicated my life to you

Defending you so much, I'd never not be right to you,

    I would never lie to you

I just wanna make sure nothing bad is gonna happen,

    I just want for you to be happy

As you're falling asleep in front of me,

    gravy is everything I ever want it be

I'll put the gravy on your mash potatoes all day long...

AESSYNCE

TOO DEEP

November 17, 2002

You're half this whole, you make me full, I couldn't exist without you now
'Cause I am you and you are you, and if you leave me now
      I wouldn't know what the hell else you would want me to do
Since the first day that I saw you it's been this thing that I believed
God put you in my life to be in your life, and I'd lose me if you leave
You are the birds, you fill my heart, you are the bee's, you are the lake
I got so much love inside of me and it's been waiting for you to take
You make me feel too deep, for this love I am a woman who is too weak
And when it's really late at night, it's what makes it so easy to fall asleep

Mentally half, emotionally half, I just couldn't be without you here
'Cause I don't know me if I don't know you and this is real, this is sincere
Because the first time I looked into your eyes I first saw him,
      I saw my man
And toward your smile, faster and faster down the hill I just ran
You satisfy my curiosity, you lead me on journey's I never knew
I explore in you to explore in me and this feeling is still the truth
You make me feel too deep, for this love I am a woman who is too weak
And when it's really late at night, it's what makes it so easy to fall asleep

We are endless, we make each other,
      we were created to be with each other
Your eyes look for me and mine check for you,

we were made to see for each other

Look at me saying things that only a grown woman could know about,

this is only what love can do

And in this union we shaped a combination,

that I could never see myself away from you

I am your feminine version, I am your half,

I am your other, I am your lover

Put it all in just one big pot,

I'll be your salt and pepper, and I'll be your butter

You make me feel too deep,

for this love every night I am a woman too weak

And when it's really late at night, it's what makes it so easy to fall asleep

You make me feel too deep...

A E S S Y N C E

-PART 3-

Under

Enough i s E n o u g h

He's been on the wrong side of right for too long
And now I have to move forward…

TRIED TO

February 2, 2003

Tried to be good, thought I loved you the best I could,
        tried to be good
Anything you asked me to I would,
        if I could do it for you I would
But it wasn't good if it didn't look like Megan Good,
        then nothing ever would
Made me feel like it wasn't good enough,
        no matter what I did it never could
You would twist me just like a doll,
        you would bake me just like a cake
And you would finger over the pretty icing
        and throw the rest of it all away
I tried to be good, thought I gave it to you the best I could,
        I did I know
I loved you with all my heart, with all my mind,
        with every ounce of my soul

Forget the hair, forget the breast, forget the purse,
        that's how real those women are
Forget about the times, forget the fights and the struggles
        'cause it's not too many women who have this heart
But it just wasn't good if it wasn't that Megan Good,

and nothing ever would
Made me feel like it just wasn't good enough,
        no matter what I did it never could
Write it all over my denim jeans,
        I was too skinny, I was too small
My hair was too short, my legs were too long,
        5'7" was just too tall
I tried to be good, thought I gave it to you the best I could,
        I did I know
I loved you with all my heart, with all my mind,
        with every ounce of my soul

Tried to be good... thought I loved you the best I could... I did, I know...

                        A E S S Y N C E

DEEP-LESS HEART

February 3, 2003

I just gotta face it, all this may have been for nothing,

    you don't feel nothing

After everything I've been going through,

    you just didn't feel me for nothing

Your ass didn't have love for me for nothing,

    you didn't appreciate me at all

While all the time your defenses were up so high,

    I was trying to break through this wall

You never gave up, you never gave in,

    you never gave anything all these days

And I never wanted you to apologize,

    somehow I always hoped you'd cave

But you didn't feed to this, you didn't eat it,

    so obvious you didn't need it

Now I gotta believe it...

you could've never fallen in love with me having a heart but so deep-less

I gotta believe it,

    you don't have no emotion, you don't feel nothing that is too soft

You wanna be so hard,

    you got so hard that you can't take that thug face off

You wanna be so thug,

    you got so hood that you don't know how to open up

While all the time that I was trying to break inside,

     there was a never a door to loosen up

I just gotta face it, you didn't seek for this,

     no future did you ever see for this

I mean from the beginning you wanted no big piece of this,

     you only tried to take it as far as a little bit

You didn't feed to this, you didn't eat it,

     you promised your best friend you didn't need it

Now I gotta believe it,

you could've never fallen in love with me having a heart but so deep-less

I gotta believe it,

     I didn't do a damn thing wrong, my love was good

And I believe it, if you were who I thought you were in the beginning

     you would've loved me with everything inside you could

So that's why I believe it,

     I didn't do a damn thing wrong, my love was true

And I pray I'll never forget what it feels like everyday

     that I use to walk through these doors and stand here next to you

I gotta believe it-

...

I swear I gotta believe it-

...

'Cause you didn't feed to this, you didn't eat it,

     you told everybody that you didn't need it

That's why I gotta believe it,

you could've never fallen in love with me having a heart but so deep-less

I gotta believe it...

                 A E S S Y N C E

Now Playing:

Blu Cantrell

>I'LL FIND A WAY

LIKE ME

February 3, 2003

Every time I think about it,

    that's the one who most deserves you

Because over again and over again

    you show me I can't be the girl for you

You cut me down, you cut me up,

    how many times I told you that's just not me

Thought that this was all I ever had,

    but now I see, in the end I still got me

TLC song in my CD player singing about a man like you,

    a man who's gots to go

So many times when I had the chance I still held on,

    I just didn't want you to go

But that's the place where you should be,

    you never wanted a love this down and deep

In the front of the whole wide world to see,

    you would've never been happy with a girl like me...

She's the one who most deserves you,

    she's everything that pleases you

So over and over I ask myself,

    why'd it take so long to eventually see the truth

I think that I deserve much more than this,

    I think in a man it should be much more than this

And even though it hurts so bad to turn around and leave,

    I need a real love much more than needing this

TLC song in my CD player singing about a man like you,

    a man that's got to go

So many times you left to go be with somebody else,

    I should've let your ass just go

'Cause that's the place where you should be,

    you never wanted a love this down and deep

In the front of all your friends to see,

    you would've never been happy with a girl like me…

So that's the girl you should've kissed,

    you couldn't handle a woman with strings attached

So that was the girl you should've hugged,

    you never lasted much more longer than that

I think that I deserve much more than that,

    I think in a man it should be much more than this

And even though it hurts so bad to turn around and leave

    I gotta believe in something much more than just all of this

That's the girl you should've shared your dances with,

    you wasn't ready for a chick so dedicated

That was the right chick you took to your house,

    you wasn't ready for a real ass woman, I gotta face it

That's the place where you should be,

    you never wanted a love this down and deep

In front of your mother and all your brothers

    you would've never been happy with a girl like me

With her is exactly where you should be…

A E S S Y N C E

BETTER OFF

February 3, 2003

Thought we had something, now I see I was wrong
Thought we'd always be together but you left and now you're gone
Maybe you're right,

    you've been saying that this would've been the better way
Maybe if we would've cut this thing a long time ago,

    letting go wouldn't be as hard as it is today
I mean I thought it would work, now it hurts me to say that it didn't work
It hurts to look back and know that loving you all this time just didn't work
I think you were right,

    maybe if we had left, maybe we'd both be much better off
Without you here, without you hurting me,

    we'd both be better off

Never thought about turning back,

    but Lord knows that things haven't been quite the same
Thought we could get love back if we just believed in that,

    but we don't even look at each other and feel the same
You could be right, so many times you said you wished we never met
You could be right, because it seems like we'd been happier by ourselves
I never thought I would say it, I never thought I could mean it, but I put in
I put in love, I put in time, everything I had to give to you I put in
But maybe you're right,

maybe if we had left that we'd both be much better off

Without you here, without you hurting me,

baby we'd both be so better off

I could think clearly for once,

with my mind no longer cluttered, my brain no longer wrecked

Maybe the grind wouldn't be as hard,

if we'd separated ourselves

You could be right,

if I want more then I would be so much better and better off

Without you here for me to love you,

baby I would be so better off...

Maybe you're right,

in time I'll see that things will eventually be alright

You say you hate the day you ever saw me

and I came in your life

But you're right,

with somebody else, I'd be so much more better off

Without you here, without you hurting me,

I'd be so much happier and better off

You're right...

A E S S Y N C E

LAST WORDS

February, 2003

I love you with a selfless, unconditional, undying love that I knew you would never be able to return. And after a while, I just grew to be happy and take whatever I could get. I would let you have your way and never put up a rebuttal. I loved you after everything you said to me and everything you said about me. I loved you throughout all the shit you did to me with an un-subtract-able emotion that we both know isn't so easy to come by. I loved you even more when it hurt me to keep on holding on and staying strong. I must've loved you more than life and anything God could put in it, even though I knew everyday that you would never be able to feel the same way about me.

I loved you and I always will. But now... I just don't love the person I am when I am with you and when I'm being in love with you. Being with you, I'm the woman who loves a man who puts his hands on her, a man who beats on her. I'm a woman in a relationship with a man who constantly cheats on her with other women and says he didn't do it, when we both know that isn't true. I'm a woman who loves a man who curses her out to her face in front of everyone she knows and publicly humiliates her. I'm this woman who loves a man too much, I'm a woman too weakened, too interrupted and broken. Always I was willing to give up my life to be in your life, and this is the way it feels like. This is the way that loving you feels...

DANGEROUSLY DEEP!!!

ENCORE

NOBODY KNOWS

September 13, 2002

Nobody knows this love that's unreturned, this fire for you that burns

Nobody sees my layers are pulling back, every corner I turn

No one feels the way I do when I can't see you and how much I miss you

And nobody hurts the way I am when I am longing to kiss you

No shoulder that I can cry on, no one to make so proud

I'm sitting here all alone, ain't no cheers for me in this crowd

Nobody says, in the end that I'm so glad that I found you

And every time I look at you, I wanna say that I'm so glad I found you too

You see nobody can taste these tears, nobody can see this shadow

Nobody can feel this pain, inside this agony it feels so hollow

No one knows, hell sometimes I don't even know as much myself

      but love chose you

And nobody hurts the way I am when I don't wanna let go of you

No side for me to stand on, no one to share my life

No hand to be my guide, ain't no where left to hide

Nobody says, in the end that I'm so glad that I found you

And every time I look at you, I wanna say that I'm so glad I found you too

Nobody knows, no one to trust, no one to talk to, ain't no company

Nobody to visit me, ain't no prison locks, nothing can set me free

No one... and not even me

And every time I look at you,

I wanna hear you say the good things you've found in me

That nobody sees and sometimes I don't see and I don't know

'Cause nobody knows and no one feels these things I've tried to just let go

Nobody says, in the end that I'm so glad that I found you

And every time I look at you, I wanna say that I'm so glad I found you too

Nobody knows…

AESSYNCE

WISHING WELL

It's so many magnificent things that will take place,
>   so much more I got for you
And I'll be your parachute through all of the turbulence
>   that you have on top of you
And to your wishes I'll be your genie,
>   and you can wish from me more wishes
And when you choose,
>   I got a phenomenal place that you can visit
I'll be your significant,
>   I'll make it my pleasure to fulfill all of your desires
And when you decide,
>   to all of your hopes I promise I will aspire
Your dreams and all your positive things,
>   pour it inside of me
Pour it inside of my wishing well,
>   pour inside of me all of your fantasies

There is nothing that I believe can stop the two of us
>   from being together
And there is no one who can come between
>   the love so strong we brought together
And to your secrets I'll be the keeper,

and when you open your eyes you'll see

Here I am and here we are,

    being everything great that great love can be

Whatever you think don't hesitate,

    don't even waste time to procrastinate

You know the type of girl I am

    don't put me on the delay

Your dreams and all your positive things,

    pour it inside of me

Pour it inside of my wishing well,

    pour inside of me all of your fantasies

Whatever you want, whatever you need, pour it inside of me...

Pour it inside of my wishing well and to your wishes I'll be the genie...

AESSYNCE

CAN'T ANYMORE

I can't chase you anymore, I can't delay it anymore

I can't pretend it anymore, like all is fine when it's so sore

I just can't do this anymore, I can't go through this anymore

I refuse this love and war that's always hurting me more

I can't live this way no more, you just can't stay here anymore

We just can't talk this out no more 'cause I don't hear you anymore

I just won't take it anymore, it's no place for me no more

I can't keep dedicating to you my riches only to be left for poor

Can't take deficiencies anymore, it's no meaning for me no more

Can't heal the hurt and pain no more, it's not a game for me no more

I'm tired, and what's going on I just can no longer ignore

Though I don't know what's all in stored, I just can't take this anymore

I cannot do this anymore, in my heart it can't be stored

'Cause you're not the kind of man that I can keep on trying and living for

I can't take this anymore, I just can't do this anymore

Won't let you lie to me anymore, won't keep on trying and trying no more

I can't, by now I'm so damn tired I know I can't

Can't take the cheating anymore, tiptoeing late night creeps no more

I can't, by now I'm so damn through I know I won't

Can't take the hiding out and finding out

      everything I hoped you wouldn't do no more

I can't, by now I'm so damn tired I know I can't

Can't take the bullsh-- anymore, argument after argument anymore

I can't, by now I'm so damn through I know I won't

Won't let you lie to me anymore, won't keep on trying and trying no more

I can't...

A E S S Y N C E

CONTACTING THE AUTHOR

Follow me on twitter
@aessynce

Add me on facebook
facebook.com/aessynce

For bookings and all other inquiries e-mail me at
aessynce_nicole@yahoo.com

7, December 2010

ISBN: 978-0-578-06690-5

www.ingramcontent.com/pod-product-compliance
Lightning Source LLC
Chambersburg PA
CBHW051829040426
42447CB00006B/439